ROTHERHAM PUBLIC LIBRARIES

This book must be returned by the date specified at the time of
issue as the Date Due for Return.
The loan may be extended (personally, by post or telephone) for
a further period, if the book is not required by another reader,
by quoting the above number   LM1 (C)

Fast and Slow

by Rod Theodorou and Carole Telford

Contents

First published in Great Britain by Heinemann Library
an imprint of Heinemann Publishers (Oxford) Ltd
Halley Court, Jordan Hill, Oxford OX2 8EJ

MADRID ATHENS PARIS FLORENCE PRAGUE WARSAW
PORTSMOUTH NH CHICAGO SAO PAULO SINGAPORE TOKYO
MELBOURNE AUCKLAND IBADAN GABORONE JOHANNESBURG

Illustrations by Sheila Townsend and Trevor Dunton
Colour reproduction by Track QSP
Printed in China

99 98 97 96
10 9 8 7 6 5 4 3 2 1

ISBN 0 431 06398 2

British Library Cataloguing in Publication Data
Telford, Carole
 Fast and Slow. – (Animal Opposites Series)
 I. Title II. Theodorou, Rod III. Series
 591.18

Photographic acknowledgements
David Fritts/OSF p4; Norbert Wu/OSF p5 *right*, back cover; Gregory G Dimijian/Photo Researchers Inc/OSF p5 *left*;
Gunter Zeisler/Bruce Coleman pp6, 8; Michael Freeman/Bruce Coleman p7; M P L Fogden/Bruce Coleman pp9,
13 *left*, 21; Gerald Cubitt/Bruce Coleman p10 *right*, back cover; David Hughes/Bruce Coleman p10 *left*; Christer
Fredriksson/Bruce Coleman p11; Paul Van Gaalen/Bruce Coleman p12; Rod Williams/Bruce Coleman p12 *insert*; Aldo
Brando/OSF p13; Steve Turner/OSF p14; Michael Fogden/OSF p15; Jen and Des Bartlett/Bruce Coleman p16;
Carol Hughes/Bruce Coleman p17; John Downer/OSF pp18, 20; Len Rue JR/Bruce Coleman p18 *insert*;
Luiz Claudio Marigo/Bruce Coleman p19
Front cover: Michael Fogden/OSF *top*; Erwin and Peggy Bauer/Bruce Coleman Ltd *bottom*

hare

falcon

cheetah

Some animals are fast.
Some animals are slow.

sloth

tortoise

snail

3

This is a
cheetah.
Cheetahs can
run very fast.

4

These are sloths.
Sloths move very
slowly.

two-toed sloth

three-toed
sloth

5

Cheetahs live on the flat
grasslands of Africa.

Sloths live among the trees in rainforests. They hardly ever come down to the ground!

Cheetahs have
long, strong legs.
They can run
faster than any other animal.

Sloths also have long, strong legs. This helps them hang upside down.

Cheetahs need to run fast to catch animals.
They have sharp teeth for ripping meat.

Sloths do not need to move fast to catch food.
They have thick lips to pluck leaves from the trees.

Cheetahs have
good eyesight.
They look out for
animals to catch
or for
enemies.

Sloths do not need good eyesight. They sleep during the day and feed at night.

13

A cheetah has sharp claws that grip the ground to help it run fast.

claws

A sloth has long
claws like hooks.
They help it hang
onto branches
all day
and all
night.

A cheetah's spotty fur helps it hide in the long grass.

A sloth's
fur is so dirty,
plants grow
in it!
A green coat
helps the sloth
stay hidden in
the trees.

A cheetah has two to five cubs
at a time.
The mother looks after them on
her own.

A sloth has
one baby at
a time.
The mother
carries the baby.

Cheetah cubs play hunting games with each other.
This helps them to learn how to hunt and kill.

Baby sloths hang onto their
mothers' fur.
This helps them grow strong arms.

AMAZING FACTS!

A cheetah is the only cat that can't pull in its claws.

Cheetahs can run at 96 kph. That's faster than a racehorse!

It can take a sloth six minutes to move the length of a bed!

Moths and beetles live in a sloth's fur!

Index